G000136874

NORMAN FERGUSON

FIRST WORLD WAR
IN THE AIR

Author's Note

The story of aviation in the First World War is a broad subject and for space reasons this book looks mainly at the British war in the air fought above the Western Front.

First published 2014

The History Press
The Mill, Brimscombe Port
Stroud, Gloucestershire, GL5 2QG
www.thehistorypress.co.uk

British Library Cataloguing in Publication Data.
A catalogue record for this book is available from the British Library.

ISBN 978 0 7509 5571 3

Typesetting and origination by The History Press
Printed in Europe

CONTENTS

INTRODUCTION

THE FIRST WORLD War was the first major conflict to see the use of aviation, initially in the form of balloons and aircraft providing aerial reconnaissance to army commanders on the ground. Aircraft were made of fabric wrapped around wooden frames; wires and wooden struts were used to brace the wings and more wires connected the pilot's controls to the ailerons, elevators and rudder. Any bullet or piece of shrapnel cutting through them would result in a swift loss of controlled flight and almost certain death.

Early aircraft were unarmed and at the start of the war opposing pilots and observers would wave as they passed each other. This soon changed: weapons started to be carried and the gentlemanly approach, harking back to medieval days of chivalry, was soon replaced by brutal aerial battles, as shockingly violent as for those in the trenches far below. Some pilots carried pistols to carry out pre-emptive action to prevent them from burning to death – parachutes were not carried, disapproved of by higher authorities for potentially impeding the aircrew's movement.

As in other conflicts, the First World War instigated innovations in technology. Aircraft in 1914 were flimsy and underpowered. With no machine guns or bomb-carrying abilities, these basic flying machines were swiftly superseded. By the last year of the war huge heavy bombers, capable of carrying a ton of bombs hundreds of miles, flew as aircraft of the new Royal Air Force, the world's first independent air service.

During the war aircraft had taken on more roles beyond flying over the battlefield on reconnaissance missions. They were now engaged in aggressive activities: bombing enemy positions, strafing trenches and shooting down aircraft, balloons and airships. At sea, aircraft flew from aircraft carriers for the first time and naval aeroplanes hunted for submarines and airships.

But these machines were no use without men to fly them. (Only a few women flew, for the military in Russia and France.) Pilots and observers were sent to squadrons with the barest of training or experience, and the resulting losses were high. These pilots were mainly unknown to the general public until the desperate need for good news from the interminable entrenched war on the Western Front allowed the press to make much of these lone aviators heading aloft in open-topped cockpits to tackle their foes in mortal combat. Those 'aces' – determined as pilots who shot down more than five enemy aircraft – were seen as the personification of individual courage; the day-to-day work carried out by the thousands of other pilots was ignored.

While the endeavours of Ball, Mannock, McCudden, Von Richthofen, Guynemer, Rickenbacker and others continue to resonate down the years, they were only one part of the first ever war in the air.

THE FIRST
MILITARY FLYERS

BRITISH MILITARY COMMANDERS were slower than their French and German counterparts to grasp the potential of aviation. From the beginning of the twentieth century, Germany had developed their huge Zeppelin airships for army and navy use and at one point just before the war Britain's military pilots numbered nineteen while France had 200.

There had been some interest shown, however. In the 1860s experiments with balloons had been carried out and the Army Balloon School had formed in 1878. Balloons were seen as potentially useful for aerial observation duties and were sent to South Africa for the Boer War. An observer raised to a decent height could see much farther than a horse-riding cavalryman; however, many of the army commanders had a cavalry background and were not overly keen on these newfangled contraptions. (They also thought aeroplanes would frighten the horses.)

DID YOU KNOW?

Geoffrey de Havilland was paid royalties for each aircraft produced from his designs. He became wealthy as a result and founded the de Havilland aircraft manufacturing company, which built the legendary Mosquito aircraft in the Second World War.

SAMUEL F. CODY

Another innovation brought to the military's attention was that of kites, able to lift soldiers or sailors to give them a high vantage point for observation purposes. The man promoting their use was Samuel F. Cody. Cody was a larger-than-life American who had run Wild West shows before turning his attention to aeronautical matters. He was also involved in the advent of airships in Britain. Britain's first military flying machine – the airship *Nulli Secundus* – first flew in 1907, with Cody having helped with the steering and engine installation.

However, it was the heavier-than-air machines, as opposed to lighter-than-air balloons and airships, that were to ensure Cody a place in aviation history. On 16 October 1908, he made Britain's first sustained and powered aircraft flight, aboard British Army Aeroplane No. 1a. At Farnborough he flew for a distance of 1,400ft and, despite crashing while trying to avoid a gorse patch, he had shown his design was capable of flight. However, the army authorities were not keen and funding was withdrawn.

I WAS THERE

Colonel Cody's Funeral
Military Honours for Dead Aviator

The high esteem held by the public for the late Mr S F Cody was demonstrated in a remarkable manner yesterday afternoon when the funeral took place at the Military Cemetery, Thornhill, Aldershot. The route from the deceased's house to the cemetery gates, a distance of two miles or more, was lined many deep by thousands of spectators.

Covered with a Union Jack the coffin was conveyed to the cemetery on a 13-pounder gun carriage. The whole of the Naval and Military Wings of the Royal Flying Corps followed, warrant and non-commissioned officers acting as bearers. On the Union Jack rested one floral tribute in the form of the steering wheel of the deceased's aeroplane but with a broken spoke. This was from the widow and bore the inscription 'In Loving Memory of my dear Frank.'

The Scotsman[1]

DID YOU KNOW?

There was a real Captain Scarlett. He was the Admiralty's Inspecting Captain of Aircraft, who evaluated aeroplanes to assess their suitability for use in the Royal Naval Air Service.

In August 1912 the Military Aviation Trials were held to select a flying machine for the Royal Flying Corps (RFC), which had been established in May that year. A prize of £4,000 was to go to the winning design. Samuel Cody's 'flying cathedral' machine (so named because of its size) won the competition but it was an outmoded design and was not put into production. Instead, the Royal Aircraft Factory's BE.2 was chosen.

EARLY TRAINING

Up until late 1914, military pilots had to pay for their own flying tuition (though if they passed the course they were reimbursed). The aeroplanes used for training were not designed for the role and some pilots learnt to fly on versions of the aircraft the Wright Brothers had made the first powered flights on. They were very unstable and notoriously difficult to fly. The first aviation fatality was an American

I WAS THERE

'L'aviation pour l'armée, c'est zéro.' (Aviation
for the army, it's worthless.)

French General Ferdinand Foch, 1910[2]

army officer killed in a Wright Brothers aircraft in 1908.

Two-seater machines weren't always available and a budding pilot would be shown what to do by an instructor, patted on the back and sent airwards on his own. A short hop would be made, then longer flights, until a student could fly a complete circuit around the airfield. If a two-seat training machine was available, the instructor would have to shout instructions over the engine noise or use a stick to get his point across more directly.

The early pilots were not fully trained in navigational techniques, such as using a compass, and instead they would follow railway lines, sometimes landing beside a station to find out where they were. Instrumentation was rudimentary: one pilot used a piece of string to tell him if he was flying level or not. Autopilot was a thing for the future and each aircraft had to be flown manually throughout the flight.

For the early aviators there was little in the way of restrictions; there was no air traffic control and they had the sky all to themselves. Pilots doing cross-country flights to improve their skills would sometimes take a week – enjoying the hospitality provided en route to these daring young men in their flying machines. These early machines were not reliable or stable, and accidents were common, but without these early pioneers willing to take to the air, the later developments would not have been possible.

FLIGHT TO WAR

IN APRIL 1911, an air battalion was formed as part of the Royal Engineers. The battalion would operate with army units in the field and use balloons, kites and aeroplanes to provide aerial reconnaissance on troop movements. It was equipped with five winged aircraft and thirty-six horses.

The battalion was to be composed of 'expert airmen' and officers would be considered if they fulfilled the following requirements:

> Special recommendation by commanding officer, possession of aviator's certificate, experience of aeronautics, rank not above captain, medically fit for air work, good eyesight, good map-reader and field sketcher, unmarried, not less than 2 years' service, under 30 years of age, good sailor, knowledge of foreign languages, taste for mechanics, light weight (under 11st 7 pounds). (Special Army Order, 28 February 1911)

DID YOU KNOW?
The Royal Flying Corps was called the Suicide Club due to the high casualty rates. More pilots and observers died in training accidents than in combat.

It was clear that one battalion would not be enough to cope with all the demands and the Royal Flying Corps was established in May 1912. It had five components:

- Military Wing
- Naval Wing
- Central Flying School
- Reserve
- Royal Aircraft Factory

The navy aviators felt their requirements were separate from the army's, and so by the time war broke out in August 1914, the naval wing had been moved under the control of the Admiralty as the Royal Naval Air Service (RNAS). As First Lord of the Admiralty, Winston Churchill was in charge of naval aviation. He had always seen the benefits of aircraft to the military – even learning to fly – and he saw to it that the Royal Naval Air Service was in charge of home defence. To this end, he stationed navy aircraft in Belgium to ward off Zeppelin attacks. This saw results when, on the night of 6 June 1915, Flight Sub-Lieutenant R.A.J. Warneford attacked and brought down Zeppelin LZ.37 near Ghent.

I WAS THERE

Airman Killed At Montrose
Biplane Turns Turtle
<u>*Pilot Falls 2000 Feet*</u>

A sad blow has been struck at aviation in Montrose, and one of the most expert young officers of the Upper Dysart Aerodrome is numbered among those who have given their lives in the attempt to conquer the air. Lieutenant Desmond L Arthur, of No 2 Squadron, Royal Flying Corps, fell from a height of 2000 feet and was killed instantaneously ... His body sank through a field of three years' grass to a depth of four feet and was frightfully mutilated. His helmet and goggles were however still on when he was discovered. The fatality is conjectured to have been the result of one of the wings failing but a report was also heard to emanate from the machine, which turned turtle, and following upon that came like a flash the apparent collapse of the aircraft.

The Scotsman.³ Lieutenant Arthur later became the subject of the wartime phenomena, known as the Montrose Ghost, when a spectre of a pilot was seen on several occasions at the Montrose airfield during the war

TO FRANCE

Shortly after war was declared, a small group of Royal Flying Corps aircraft flew to France to support the British Expeditionary Force (BEF) as they faced the German Army, which was advancing through Belgium towards France. The first aircraft touched down at 8.20 a.m. on 13 August 1914, flown by Major Hubert Harvey-Kelly of 2 Squadron. Four squadrons arrived – 2, 3, 4 and 5 – with a mixture of types: BE.2as, Avro 504s, Farmans and Bleriot monoplanes (the latter was the same type that had first flown the English Channel five years previously). Sixty-three aircraft were flown over. Airfields

DID YOU KNOW?

The iconic 'Mod' roundel came from the war. British aircraft originally carried no nationality markings and were fired on by their own side's troops: at least one Royal Flying Corps aircraft was shot down by French troops. To improve identification, Union Jacks were painted on the undersides of the wings, but at a distance they resembled the Iron Crosses painted on the German aircraft. The circular roundel design was adopted, based on that of the French air force, but with blue on the outside, then white and red bull's eye.

were few in number and suitable land had to be negotiated with local farmers. Pilots had to avoid hitting the cows that had remained on one Royal Flying Corps airfield.

FIRST VICTORY

These first British war machines were unarmed and crews had to carry whatever armament they had to hand, such as revolvers and rifles. On 25 August 1914, the Royal Flying Corps shot down its first German aircraft, a Taube monoplane, hit with bullets fired by Lieutenant Euan Rabagliati of 5 Squadron using a rifle.

RECONNAISSANCE

The main role of the Royal Flying Corps was to provide aerial reconnaissance. Not all in higher command saw the need for aircraft, but General Haig, who was later to command the whole of the British Army on the Western Front, had experience of the effectiveness of airpower. During a pre-war exercise, his opponent made better use of aircraft in spotting troop movements and won the day.

In the battles for real, the first British airmen showed their worth in the retreat from Mons and at the subsequent Battle of the Marne in September 1914. They were able to spot German troops and relay the information back to HQ, where it could be acted on. With the trenches being dug in late 1914, and the war not about to be finished by Christmas, the Royal Flying Corps would have to adapt to flying in a war of attrition no one had planned for.

DID YOU KNOW?

The last surviving pilot of the Royal Flying Corps died in 2002. Hubert Williams joined in 1915 and said of his time in the corps: 'I'm no hero – I just consider myself a remarkably lucky man to have survived.' He had been shot down in Macedonia. He was 106 when he died.

EYES IN THE SKY

THE EARLY BRITISH aircrews struggled to gain appreciation of the usefulness of aerial reconnaissance. In the first days of the war, one pilot's report was mistakenly dismissed by a senior general. The pilots and observers persevered and their value was proven when aircraft revealed the exposed position of British troops after the Battle of Mons. After trenches were established on the Western Front, there was no longer the need to scout for mass movements of troops and equipment across the battlefield. Instead, aircraft would overfly fixed enemy positions looking for potential weak points to attack. They would also search for concentrations of troops, indicating an imminent attack.

THE AIRCRAFT

As reconnaissance was the main role of the Royal Flying Corps, they were keen to have aircraft that were stable, allowing the aircrew to make notes and sketches easily on a straight and level course. The RE.8 biplane was so steady that when the pilot and observer of one plane were killed their aircraft continued to fly on, travelling 30 miles before slowly descending to the ground. However, a slow and steady aircraft was not suited to the quick turning manoeuvres required for aerial combat, and they proved vulnerable to enemy fighters.

OBSERVATION

At first, only visual observation was carried out. This meant having to fly relatively low, which brought the aircraft within range of enemy rifle and machine-gun fire. As aircraft flew higher to escape, they moved out of range for the naked eye to take in details, even with binoculars. Also, with visual observation, only so much information could be gathered. A more accurate record was needed, and photography was brought in to achieve this.

DID YOU KNOW?

The Royal Flying Corps' standard reconnaissance aircraft from 1917, the RE.8 biplane, was given the rhyming nickname 'Harry Tate' after a music hall entertainer.

I WAS THERE

I wish particularly to bring to your Lordships' notice the admirable work done by the Royal Flying Corps under Sir David Henderson. Their skill, energy, and perseverance have been beyond all praise. They have furnished me with the most complete and accurate information which has been of incalculable value in the conduct of the operations.

Sir John French, Commander British Expeditionary Force, September 1914, dispatch to Secretary of State for War[4]

PHOTOGRAPHIC RECONNAISSANCE

The first cameras were bulky, heavy and had to be held over the side of the fuselage. Glass plates were used to record the image and these had to be changed manually each time a picture was taken – a task made harder with the aeroplane being buffeted by enemy anti-aircraft fire. Eventually cameras were mounted on the sides of the aircraft's fuselage, and mechanisms were introduced that could wind on the plates.

Once developed and analysed back at HQ, the images showed enemy positions in great detail. Individual soldiers could be seen, and a good photographic interpreter could even tell if a train was loaded or empty. They could also spot artillery guns through camouflage. Through photography, a map was produced of the whole trench system.

DID YOU KNOW?

500,000 aerial reconnaissance photographs were taken by the British.

I WAS THERE

4.02pm *A very little short. Fire. Fire.*

4.04pm *Fire again. Fire again.*

4.12pm *A little short; line OK.*

4.15pm *Short. Over, over and a little left.*

4.20pm *You were just between two batteries.
Search two hundred yards each side
of your last shot. Range OK.*

4.22pm *You have them.*

4.26pm *Hit. Hit. Hit.*

4.32pm *About 50 yards short and to the right.*

4.37pm *Your last shot in the middle of 3
batteries in action; search all round
within 300 yards of your last
shot and you have them.*

4.42pm *I am coming home now.*

*Royal Flying Corps artillery observation aircraft
to a battery in the first use of airborne radio in
warfare, 24 September 1914*[5]

ARTILLERY OBSERVATION

Another vital task was helping the army's artillery batteries find their targets. Flying thousands of feet in the air, a spotter could see the fall of shot relatively easily. Range and accuracy information was passed down by lights, flags, flares, and then by wireless messages sent via Morse code. The first wireless transmitters were so heavy that the observer couldn't go up and the pilot had to send the signals himself, while also flying the aircraft. The airborne radio sets only worked one way, so the artillery batteries had to send their message skywards using large cloth strips laid out on the ground.

One drawback of artillery observation was having to fly close to the shells' trajectories. One pilot watched fascinatedly as a large howitzer shell went past him at 8,000ft as it slowly reached the top of its arc. He was lucky: others were killed by their own side's shells.

DID YOU KNOW?

In 1918 the Germans introduced a reconnaissance aircraft capable of flying at 24,000ft. The Rumpler C VII used an automated camera but the crews suffered decompression sickness (the bends, normally associated with deep-sea divers) when descending.

CONTACT PATROLS

Keeping the generals up to date with the progress of an offensive was always difficult in the heat of battle, and one way of doing this was to carry out contact patrols. Aircraft flew low over the battlefield, watching for signs from troops indicating their position, which the aircrews would report back to HQ. The aircraft would announce their arrival over their assigned sector by blowing klaxon horns. Troops below were then to light smoke candles, flares or wave their hats from the tips of their bayonets. Mirrors were even attached to soldiers' backs to reflect sunlight to make them easier to spot. Understandably, troops were not keen to give away their position in ways that could be easily seen by the enemy, but contact patrols proved useful to army chiefs.

The work of the reconnaissance aircrews was vital, so much so that no offensive was started unless a thorough aerial reconnaissance had been undertaken beforehand.

THE FIRST BATTLE
OF BRITAIN

ON THE NIGHT of 19 January 1915, the nightmare dreaded by many became a reality, as German Zeppelins mounted their first raid on Britain. These giant airships – some over 600ft long – could carry 2 tons of bombs from their bases on the Continent, and their range meant that they could attack anywhere in Britain.

Fears of an aerial onslaught had been raised in 1908, when novelist H.G. Wells published his novel *War in the Air*. It depicted an apocalyptic future where cities could be devastated by German airships. Outrage had been caused at the start of the war when the Belgian city of Antwerp had been bombed. Now it was Britain's turn. Four were killed in the first attack and, when London was first targeted in May 1915, seven died.

DID YOU KNOW?

The legendary cricketer W.G. Grace is reputed to have died as a result of a Zeppelin raid. When an airship went over, he would stand outside his south London home, shaking his fist and shouting. During one raid in 1915 he collapsed from a stroke and died a week later.

DEFENCE MEASURES

Despite the German airships' size, they were not easy to detect, especially at night, which was when the raids took place. While they were hard to spot (nine out of ten home defence pilots never even saw one in the air), they were even harder to bring down, as Britain's defences were poorly prepared for aerial attack. The aircraft available had no armament, unless the crew carried their own pistols or rifles, which were wholly inadequate against an airship. When machine guns were fitted, it was found that the ammunition wouldn't ignite the airship's hydrogen to destroy it. Bombs were tried, but they would fall right through the airship if they didn't hit anything to detonate against.

More effective measures had to be found. One experiment was the Fiery Grapnel. It required the pilot to fly over the airship, lower a grapnel hook by rope and allow it to rip open the fabric skin, whereby an explosive charge would be set off. Described as 'suicidal', they were never put into operational use. However, some squadron commanders were so determined to stop the Zeppelins that they felt pilots should ram them in mid-air.

Matters improved by 1916, and searchlights, anti-aircraft guns and aircraft were organised to form a competent defence force. Detection of the airships' radio signals allowed their position to be plotted, and when aircraft began to be equipped with incendiary and explosive ammunition there was an increase in their effectiveness. These bullets could ignite the hydrogen, and in September 1916, the first German airship was brought down on British soil by Lieutenant William Leefe Robinson, using the new bullets. Thousands gathered to watch the flaming airship fall to the ground and Robinson became a household name.

'HEIGHT CLIMBERS'

As the effectiveness of the home defences began to tell, a new form of airship was introduced by the Germans. These were known as 'Height Climbers', designed to reach 20,000ft – well above the altitude capability of British fighters. Their crews suffered from the lack of oxygen and bitter cold, and several were shot down by British fighters; airship attacks were curtailed in 1917.

Out of the 115 Zeppelins employed in the war, 77 were put out of action.

I WAS THERE

Public Warning

Should hostile aircraft be seen, take shelter immediately in the nearest available house, preferably in the basement, and remain there until the aircraft have left the vicinity: do not stand about in crowds and do not touch unexploded bombs.

Advice from aircraft recognition poster

GOTHAS AND GIANTS

While it was the Zeppelins that had attracted the attention of the military and the civilian population, there was a second, more destructive element to the Germans' aerial arsenal: long-range bomber aircraft.

The first inkling of this new wave of terror from the skies came on 25 May 1917, when twenty-one Gotha bombers attacked Britain. They killed 95 and injured almost 200 at Folkestone and the army camp at Shorncliffe. Only one of the bombers was shot down, on its return flight over the English Channel.

As with the Zeppelin raids, the British capital was the prize target, and on 13 June 1917, twenty Gothas attacked London. They hit Liverpool Street railway station and an infants' school, killing sixteen young children. In total for the raid, 162 people were killed and 432 injured, some by shrapnel caused by British anti-aircraft fire. The capital's defences were not up to the job and each bomber returned to its base unscathed. Another large raid on 7 July killed fifty-seven civilians.

I WAS THERE

Zeppelin's Fate at Dawn

Suddenly the gunfire ceased and almost immediately a vivid flash of light leaped from the side of the airship. 'She's hit' shouted the crowd on the cliffs, and a great cheer rang through the still and frosty air. Within a few seconds, the Zeppelin was a mass of golden-red flames. The blazing frame tilted slowly over and then dived swiftly to the sea, leaving in its wake a long pillar of dense smoke, which showed strangely against the increasing light of dawn.

Account of attack on Zeppelin L.21 by anti-aircraft artillery and naval aircraft off the coast of East Anglia[6]

DID YOU KNOW?

A total of 4,830 British people were killed or wounded by German air raids. In an effort to quell public anxiety, it was revealed that, compared to those killed in London by enemy action, far more had died in road traffic accidents.

DEFENCES

There was a clamour for action and London's defences were strengthened: fighter squadrons were ordered back from France. The public was alerted to incoming air raids: policemen cycled around ringing bells, shouting warnings and blowing whistles. As in the Second World War, the London Underground provided a safe haven – 300,000 people taking shelter below the streets was not uncommon – and casualties were reduced. The defences saw success and an attack in August 1917 saw three Gothas lost to fighters and anti-aircraft fire. German commanders decreed that raids would take place at night from then on.

NIGHT RAIDS

In September 1917, the Gothas carried out their first night-time air raid. Chatham naval base was the target and 130 naval recruits were killed when their barracks were hit. The following night, London was targeted and nineteen were killed. Night raids meant a bigger headache for the defence fighters and it wasn't until December that a British night fighter shot down a Gotha.

FINAL ATTACK

The last, and biggest, aircraft raid of the war was on 19/20 May 1918, when forty-one Gothas and the larger Giant bombers attacked London, killing forty-nine people. The air raids on Britain had shown the difficulties in combating aerial attacks, and these problems would still need to be overcome when the next Battle of Britain took place in 1940.

DID YOU KNOW?

Three times as many people were killed in towns and cities outside of London during the Zeppelin period of bombing.

I WAS THERE

*It is far better to face the bullets than to be
killed at home by a bomb.
Join the army at once and help to stop an air raid.
God save the King.*

British recruiting poster

FIGHTERS

THE WAR BEGAN without fighter aircraft. Aeroplanes were seen mainly as aerial observation platforms and it was only when their usefulness grew, and with it the enemy's desirability to shoot them down, that the concept of aerial battles featuring aeroplane *v.* aeroplane began. Reconnaissance and artillery observation aircraft would have to defend themselves as best they could against enemy attackers until escorting fighters could be brought into service.

SUITABILITY

The early machines were underpowered and intended for steady flying, and therefore were not suitable for the rapid climbing, diving and turning needed for fighter attacks. Aircraft were prone to come apart if they engaged in too strenuous manoeuvres. The other part of the problem for the designers was the armament. The rifles, pistols and sawn-off shotguns that were carried by the pilots and observers at first were of limited use in downing enemy aircraft. Machine guns had a high enough rate of fire to be able to give a better chance of landing bullets on a fast-moving target, but they were heavy and slowed down the already cumbersome machines. Crews would watch as German aircraft pulled out of range.

TYPES

There were two main types of aircraft.

'Tractor' machines had the engine and propeller at the front, 'pulling' the aircraft through the air. This meant a machine gun couldn't be fitted to fire straight ahead or it would just blast the wooden propeller to pieces. Guns could be mounted on top of the higher wing, but this meant the pilot had to stand up precariously on his seat to reload the magazines. Some pilots mounted their guns on the fuselage to shoot out at an angle, but this presented considerable aiming difficulties. Two-seater tractor aircraft had a machine gun that the observer operated. Its range of fire was limited – its forward firing was non-existent – and if not properly aimed, the gun risked shooting off the tail fin.

DID YOU KNOW?

Although giving personal names to aircraft is associated with the Second World War, machines were also personalised in the First. These names were given to Sopwith Pup fighter aircraft: *Baby Mine, Betty, Bobs, Brandy, Chin-Chow, Happy, Julia, Mildred H, Mina, Normie, Otazel, Will-o'-the-Wisp, Wonga!*

I WAS THERE

There are no aeroplanes with the Royal Flying Corps really suitable for carrying machine-guns; grenades and bombs are therefore at present most suitable. If suitable aeroplanes are available, machine-guns are better undoubtedly. Request you to endeavour to supply efficient fighting machines as soon as possible.

General David Henderson, Commander Royal Flying Corps, 4 September 1914[7]

'Pushers' had the engine mounted behind the pilot and observer. This afforded the observer, who sat in the front, a perfectly clear firing position forwards, but it also meant he was vulnerable to attack from head on. His field of fire rearwards was handicapped by the position of the engine, and many pushers were downed by attacks from behind without ever seeing their opponent.

Aircraft manufacturers produced many different designs throughout the war (over 380 different marks of military aircraft were built by all countries), although it took a few years for true fighters, designed from the start to bring down enemy aircraft, to equip squadrons. They were made to be faster and nimbler, but it was difficult to get the right balance and there was much debate amongst pilots whether speed and rate of climb was more important than manoeuvrability. A strongly built aircraft could survive more punishment at the expense of being able to turn quickly.

SYNCHRONISATION GEAR

The real breakthrough came with the introduction of synchronisation gear. It was found that the best way to shoot down an aircraft was to have a fixed gun pointing forwards and have the pilot fly until it was pointed at the target. French pilot Roland Garros had devised a method of fixing metal plates to his aircraft's propeller to allow machine-gun bullets to pass through. It proved successful and he shot down three German machines, but when he himself was shot down the Germans were able to find out this secret and use it to develop their own forward-firing equipment. Their synchronisation gear would only allow the machine gun to fire when the propeller was out of the way and it was first fitted on to their Fokker Eindecker fighters.

AIR SUPREMACY

The air war saw both sides battle for supremacy. Germany, with its Fokker Eindeckers, gained the upper hand in 1915 and into 1916, then the Allies with their Nieuports, DH.2s and FE.2bs were able to help redress the balance in the spring of that year, and then, during the Battle of the Somme from July onwards, with the arrival of aircraft like the Sopwith Pup. The German Albatros D-series fighters, with their two machine guns, started to enter service in the middle of 1916 and ruled the skies from the latter part of that year into

1917, until the SE.5a, Bristol fighter and Sopwith Camel battled to give the Allies a hard-fought advantage to the end of the war, despite the Germans having their squadrons equipped with the impressive Fokker D.VII.

DOGFIGHTS

Battles between machines were termed 'dogfights'. Aircraft twisted and turned, trying to gain an advantage to fire the lethal shots. One notable dogfight was between Royal Flying Corps ace Lanoe Hawker and Manfred von Richthofen. It lasted twenty minutes and only ended when Hawker made a dash for base with his fuel running low. Hawker was as skilled as any pilot, but he was unable to get away: one of Richthofen's bullets hit him in the head, killing him instantly.

Although dogfights captured the imagination, many aircraft were shot down in a short space of time. Fighters would swoop down, firing short bursts, and then pull away. Some never saw their attacker, the pursuing aircraft closing to within feet behind them before opening fire. As the war went on, individual battles became rare as air fighting became more organised and big formations would face up to each other in large melees.

I WAS THERE

I saw him go into a fairly steep dive and so I continued to watch, and then saw the triplane hit the ground and disappear into a thousand fragments, for it seemed to me that it literally went into powder.

James McCudden, describing the shooting down of German ace Werner Voss, which took place on 23 September 1917[8]

DID YOU KNOW?

One of the Royal Naval Air Service pilots who shot down Zeppelin LZ.61 in November 1916 was Flight Lieutenant Egbert Cadbury. He was heir to the chocolate manufacturing empire and survived the war to become its managing director.

GROUND ATTACK

Nimble fighter planes were suitable for another task: ground attack. Pilots returning from operations would drop down and strafe the enemy trenches with machine-gun fire. In September 1916, one trench full of over 350 Germans surrendered en masse after being attacked in this way. According to H.A. Jones in *The War in the Air*, a German officer said that Allied planes had 'seized [his troops] with a fear almost amounting to a panic'. Ground attack sorties became more organised and, co-ordinated with infantry and artillery attacks, were used to great effect in the Allies' offensives of 1918.

BOMBERS

AS WAS THE situation with fighters, when the war began there were no dedicated bomber aircraft on the strength of the British air forces. Even the navy, which had carried out pre-war experiments on aerial bombing, only had twenty-six bombs available. One of these experiments explored safe separation distances for aircraft dropping bombs. Explosive charges floating on the sea were set off while aircraft passed overhead at different heights. Fortunately, the tests were successful and no aircraft or pilots were damaged.

Once war began, the experimentation continued. Fourteen-inch-long darts, known as 'flechettes', were tried as weapons, although without much success. Hand grenades were used, manually thrown out of cockpits or dropped down improvised tubes. Not all managed to drop clear and anxious crews would return to base with a pinless grenade wedged feet away. Artillery shells were flung over the side before bombs as we know them were introduced. Even then there were no bombsights and pilots had to fly as low as they dared to try to reach some measure of accuracy. Their efforts were literally hit or miss.

ANTI-ZEPPELIN MISSIONS

When the First World War began, the German Zeppelins were regarded as the main bombing threat to Britain. As aircraft struggled to intercept them in the air, Royal Naval Air Service aircraft were sent to destroy Zeppelins on the ground, and so the first British bombing raids were carried out by the Royal Navy.

A plan was drafted and the first air raid on Germany took place in September 1914, when the Zeppelin sheds at Cologne and Dusseldorf were attacked. Four land-based aircraft took part, all of different types. One was a Sopwith Sociable, which was not a greatly appropriate name for a weapon of war. Only one machine found the target and caused some minor injuries to German troops. The bombs the aircraft carried weighed 20lb, only 4½lb of which was explosive charge.

DID YOU KNOW?

In the midst of German air raids by Gotha bombers in 1917, it was felt insensitive for the Royal Family to have a Germanic name; thus Saxe-Coburg-Gotha was dropped and Windsor adopted.

I WAS THERE

The attack on Libercourt deserves special mention for it was conducted with much skill and audacity. The object was to interrupt traffic on the railway from Lille to Douai. Trains were running south carrying reserves or munitions for the battle of the Somme ... Captain C and his machine gunner Sergeant J descended to about 800 feet over the first train and successfully dropped 6 bombs. The engine was hit and jumped the rails. Three coaches were telescoped and the maddened German soldiers got out of the carriages looking for a way of escape towards Ostricourt and in the direction of woods nearby. But Captain C went still lower, fired on the disorganised crowd leaving numerous dead and wounded on the ground.

French report on a British bombing mission, issued 3 October 1916[5]

The next month a more successful mission took place during which a Zeppelin was destroyed by bombs dropped by a Sopwith Tabloid biplane at Dusseldorf. The aircraft didn't have enough fuel to return to its Antwerp base and after making a forced landing the pilot returned by bicycle.

Another raid took place on 21 November, when the Zeppelin sheds at Friedrichshafen were bombed by three Royal Naval Air Service Avro 504 biplanes. It was a long-distance flight – 125 miles – to the target on Lake Constance, which bordered Austria. It was a risky endeavour: the pilots had never dropped a bomb before. One of them took his machine down to 10ft as he approached the target over the lake, a height six times lower than the Dambusters would fly in 1943. How much damage was caused by this daring mission was difficult to ascertain, but these raids showed what was possible by aerial bombing.

DID YOU KNOW?

Italy was the first country to conduct bombing from the air. In a dispute with the Ottoman Empire over territory in Libya in 1911, the first aerial weapon to be used in anger was a hand grenade dropped by an Italian officer on a military camp.

I WAS THERE

A Little Hell(P) From the RAF

Message written on 1,650lb bomb, August 1918

DEVELOPMENTS

By 1916, bombing by the Royal Flying Corps had become more organised, with massed formations attacking valuable targets such as railway junctions, airfields and troop barracks. Bombers were now able to influence the outcome of battles. Bombsights had been introduced and were sorely needed: in one four-month period in 1915, only three Allied bombing raids on railway stations out of 141 were successful.

Bombing by day meant a better chance of accuracy at a higher risk of attracting the attention of enemy fighters and anti-aircraft fire. The vulnerable, heavily laden bombers were described in Walter Raleigh's *The War in the Air* as being 'cold meat' for enemy fighters. Bombing at night was introduced. It reduced the chances of being hit, but meant decreased chances of hitting the target. Losses were high, as an aggressive policy was followed of attacking the enemy at all times.

DID YOU KNOW?
British air forces dropped 8,000 tons of bombs during the First World War.

STRATEGIC BOMBING

Germany led the way in bombing strategic targets such as major cities, but following the Gotha raids on Britain in 1917, reprisal raids on Germany were ordered. The Royal Naval Air Service had built up experience of strategic bombing and had the foresight to order large heavy bombers, which appeared in the shape of the Handley Page 0/100 and the 0/400. These could carry six times the bomb load of the Royal Flying Corps' DH.4s and were Britain's first heavy bombers. Together, these machines, with some other types such as FE.2ds, bombed factories, railway yards, munitions works, barracks, power stations, docks, airfields and steelworks. It was an intensive campaign: in June 1918 there were only six nights when Germany wasn't targeted. Berlin was to be raided, but the war ended before this symbolic attack could be carried out.

ALLIED AIRCRAFT

IN AUGUST 1914, Britain lagged behind its Continental neighbours. France's air force had 160 aircraft, Germany 282, while Britain's Royal Flying Corps sent sixty-three to the Continent. The increasing roles required more and varied types to be designed and built, and manufacturers responded. These are some of the more notable aircraft produced by the Allies.

RUSSIA

Ilya Muromets

Introduced: 1914
Speed: 68mph
Maximum altitude: 10,000ft

Used to bomb German forces on the Eastern Front, this four-engined giant – its wings spanned 105ft – was the world's first heavy bomber. It had nine machine guns and racks to carry 1,800lb of bombs. Only one was lost to German fighter planes, whose pilots were anxious about attacking such a well-defended machine.

DID YOU KNOW?

The world's first fighter squadron was British: 11 Squadron RFC, which operated from July 1915.

BRITAIN

Royal Aircraft Factory BE.2c
Introduced: February 1915
Speed: 72mph
Maximum altitude: 10,000ft
BE.2s were produced in large numbers – around 3,500 were built – and supplied to front-line squadrons even when obsolete. They were used for reconnaissance, bombing and anti-Zeppelin missions: a BE.2c brought down the first Zeppelin to be shot down over Britain. They were slow and cumbersome, making them 'Fokker fodder' for the German fighters.

Royal Aircraft Factory FE.2b
Introduced: September 1915
Speed: 91mph
Maximum altitude: 11,500ft
A two-seater 'pusher', the FE.2b was used as a fighter aircraft. It had two machine guns: one that fired forward and another that fired backwards over the wing. To use it the observer had to stand precariously in the open cockpit, his knees above the cockpit edge. 'Fees' were effective and German ace Max Immelmann was shot down by one. Later versions operated as bombers right up to the end of the war.

Airco DH.2
Introduced: February 1916
Speed: 93mph
Maximum altitude: 14,500ft
Britain's first purpose-built fighter. The DH.2 was a single-seater and the pilot operated the one machine gun, which, as the aircraft was a 'pusher' type, was mounted on the very front of the fuselage. DH.2s were welcomed at the front line where, along with the FE.2b, they helped overcome the 'Fokker scourge' of late 1915 and early 1916.

Sopwith Pup
Introduced: September 1916
Speed: 111mph
Maximum altitude: 17,500ft
The Pup had excellent handling characteristics, especially at altitude, and was popular with its pilots. One pilot described it as 'the perfect flying machine'.[10] Over 1,700 were made, and a Pup made the very first landing on a moving aircraft carrier.

Airco DH.4
Introduced: March 1917
Speed: 143mph
Maximum altitude: 22,000ft

The DH.4 was used for bombing and artillery observation by the Royal Flying Corps and later by the US Army Air Service. Despite being known as the Flaming Coffin for its tendency to catch fire, it was seen as the best single-engine day bomber of the war. It could fly at high altitude with no fighter escorts, carrying 460lb of bombs on underwing racks. The Royal Naval Air Service also used DH.4s and sank a U-boat with them in August 1918.

Bristol F.2b Fighter

Introduced: April 1917

Speed: 125mph

Maximum altitude: 20,000ft

On its first appearance over the battlefield, the two-seater 'Brisfit' encountered Albatroses led by legendary German fighter pilot Manfred von Richthofen – the Red Baron. Four were shot down, one of which was flown by Captain Leefe Robinson, who had shot down the first German airship over Britain. The pilots were under the impression that the aircraft was not that sturdy and flew it too gently. Once they realised how strong and manoeuvrable it was, they operated it as a fighter and it became a valuable part of the Royal Flying Corps' inventory, and then the Royal Air Force's, being flown until the 1930s.

I WAS THERE

What I want is a bloody paralyser not a toy.

Commodore Murray Seuter, Director of the Admiralty Air Department, to Frederick Handley Page[11]

DID YOU KNOW?

The most produced aircraft of the war was the Avro 504, with almost 9,000 built. Despite its unfortunate place in history as the first Royal Flying Corps aircraft shot down in the war, it gave great service, being used to bomb Friedrichshafen in 1914, before becoming outdated and used as a trainer.

Royal Aircraft Factory SE.5a

Introduced: April 1917

Speed: 138mph

Maximum altitude: 20,000ft

One of the war's best fighters. It was fast, had good manoeuvrability and was also stable enough to be flown by inexperienced pilots. It was equipped with two machine guns: a Vickers firing through the propeller and a Lewis on top of the wing. In order to reload the Lewis gun, the pilot pulled it back down towards him, the gun being on a curved rail. This meant it could also be aimed and fired in an upwards direction, which pilots like Albert Ball used to attack enemy aircraft from beneath.

Sopwith Camel

Introduced: June 1917

Speed: 117mph

Maximum altitude: 19,000ft

Britain's most successful fighter of the war: Camels shot down 1,294 enemy aircraft. They were not easy to fly, being described by one pilot as 'a fierce little beast',[12] and 798 British pilots were killed flying them, most in training accidents. The gyroscopic effects of its rotary engine meant it could turn twice as quickly to the right as to the left. This was a useful attribute in combat, but if not controlled properly it could easily lead to a spin. In August 1918 there were more Camel squadrons than any other aircraft in the Royal Flying Corps.

Handley Page 0/400

Introduced: early 1918

Speed: 98mph

Maximum altitude: 8,500ft

The 0/400 was a development of the 0/100, which was the biggest aircraft Britain had produced, with a wingspan of 100ft. The Royal Naval Air Service had ordered a heavy strategic bomber in order to attack targets inside Germany and these giant machines were able to carry a bomb weighing 1,650lb. Over

400 0/400s were built. They undertook night raids into Germany as part of the Independent Force — bombers employed against strategic targets as opposed to those near to the battlefields.

FRANCE

Nieuport 17
Introduced: March 1916
Speed: 110mph
Maximum altitude: 17,400ft
At one point in 1916, the nimble Nieuport 17 equipped every French fighter squadron. British ace Albert Ball hung on to his Nieuport even when the SE.5a was brought into service.

SPAD XIII
Introduced: May 1917
Speed: 135mph
Maximum altitude: 22,400ft
The SPADs were fast and strong, able to dive on to a target and get away quickly. Eight thousand five hundred SPAD XIIIs were built, and when the USA joined the war, as it had no aircraft of its own, it received almost 900 of them.

I WAS THERE

Nothing would induce me to leave the floor on which I was sitting. I simply felt too scared to move.

A FE.2b observer on his first flight[13]

GERMAN AIRCRAFT

GERMANY PRODUCED MANY notable aircraft and its fighters often had the upper hand. It arguably produced the best fighting aircraft of the war in the Fokker D.VII.

Etrich Taube
Introduced: 1910
Speed: 72mph
Maximum altitude: 9,800ft
The Taube (Dove) had a distinctive bird-like shape. Unarmed, it was used for reconnaissance, although one was known as 'The Five O'Clock Taube' for its regularity in bombing Paris in 1914. It did this twelve times, killing and wounding over sixty people.

Fokker Eindecker
Introduced: summer 1915
Speed: 87mph
Maximum altitude: 11,500ft
The Eindecker monoplane was the first fighter to be equipped with the revolutionary ability to fire forwards through the propeller. The first Allied aircraft that encountered them were surprised to be fired on by an aeroplane heading towards them and didn't take defensive action quickly enough. Flown by German aces Oswald Boelcke and Max

Immelmann, the Eindeckers gave their name to the period of German air supremacy: the 'Fokker scourge'.

Gotha IV

Introduced: February 1917
Speed: 87mph
Maximum altitude: 21,300ft
Gothas were the most numerous of Germany's heavy bombers. Twin-engined, they had a crew of three: pilot, observer/bomb aimer/front gunner and rear gunner. The aircraft included a clever arrangement whereby the gunner could fire through the bottom of the fuselage, thus surprising British pilots who had been told that this was the best place to attack.

Zeppelin-Staaken R.VI

Introduced: June 1917
Speed: 81mph
Maximum altitude: 14,000ft
Germany's biggest operational bomber. The R.VI – R for 'Riesenflugzeuge' (giant aircraft) – was twice as big as a Gotha, and had a wingspan 36ft longer than a Second World War Avro Lancaster. Two mechanics sat in the engine nacelles. The R.VI could carry 2 tons of bombs. No 'Giant' was shot down over Britain.

I WAS THERE

The German army possesses war Tauben which are not however employed as carrier pigeons, but are used for destroying the enemy's aeroplanes and airships. These pigeons are so trained that they seek their food on the wings of aeroplanes and airships. A small bomb is tied round the neck of these pigeons which are then sent out and flying over the hostile aeroplane alights on the planes of it, the bomb being caused to explode by the impact of alighting. This explosion is sufficient to put the aeroplane out of action, or to ignite the gas of an airship. The pigeon, of course, pays with its life for its unconsciously warlike action.

Story from a Czech newspaper[14]

DID YOU KNOW?

Germany produced over 44,000 aircraft during the war, as opposed to the 107,000 made by Britain and France.

Albatros D.V

Introduced: July 1917

Speed: 116mph

Maximum altitude: 20,500ft

The Albatros D-series of fighter aircraft were powerful and equipped with two machine guns. They dominated the skies with their superior firepower and speed, but the D-series had a flaw: the wings were prone to structural failure and pilots were forbidden from sustained dives in case the wings broke off. Over 4,500 Albatroses were made.

Fokker Dr.1 Triplane

Introduced: August 1917

Speed: 103mph

Maximum altitude: 20,000ft

German designers were so impressed by the British Sopwith Triplane that they built their own three-winged fighter. It was light, could turn quickly and could appear to hang in the air, firing upwards as Allied planes tried to escape. Manfred von Richthofen shot down nineteen of his kills in his specially painted red Dr.1, and its phenomenal climbing ability meant he could lift himself out of any dogfight whenever he felt threatened. It was succeeded by the Fokker D.VII.

Fokker D.VII
Introduced: early 1918
Speed: 124mph
Maximum altitude: 23,000ft
Germany's fighters were becoming outmoded at the start of 1918 and squadron pilots were delighted to receive their new aircraft. Fast, manoeuvrable and with good handling, it was one of the very best fighters of the First World War. Forty squadrons were flying the D.VII by the latter stages of the war.

DID YOU KNOW?

The Fokker D.VII was seen as such a threat that it was the only aircraft mentioned by name in the Armistice agreement that ended the war in November 1918.

I WAS THERE

I must say that the Albatros, when climbing steeply, is a very comic sight, for normally it flies rather tail low, and when it is up about 12,000 feet climbing at 60 mph, at which speed they do climb efficiently, it always gives me the impression of a small dog begging.

Major James McCudden, VC, Royal Flying Corps[15]

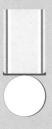

THE AIR ACES

THE FIGHTER PILOTS' individual exploits gained focus that helped take the public's attention away from the war of attrition being fought in the trenches. These are some of the most well known.

FRANCE

Rene Fonck
75 kills
France's highest-scoring ace, Fonck was not regarded with affection due to a perceived aloof and boastful nature. However, he was a skilful pilot and marksman who shot down six enemy aircraft in one day on more than one occasion. A careful pilot, he was never wounded during the war and died in 1953.

Georges Guynemer
53 kills
France's second-highest scoring pilot, Guynemer was deemed too frail to serve in the infantry – he only weighed 132lb – but in flying a lightweight fighter aeroplane, this was not a hindrance. During one dogfight his Nieuport landed with eighty-six bullet holes, but in September 1917 his luck ran out and his SPAD

crashed in no-man's-land. French children were taught that their hero had flown so high he couldn't return to earth.

Charles Nungesser
45 kills
The dashing Nungesser was renowned for continuing to fly despite his many injuries. Following one bad crash, in which he broke both legs, he resumed flying using crutches to get to his aircraft. He disappeared while attempting a transatlantic flight in 1927.

CANADA

Raymond Collishaw
60 kills
Navy pilot Collishaw flew Sopwith Pups, Triplanes, then Camels. He led the renowned 'Black Flight' – so named because each of its five aeroplanes were painted black. The all-Canadian flight was highly successful, shooting down eighty-seven aircraft in just two months in the summer of 1917. Collishaw continued to serve in the Royal Air Force into the Second World War.

I WAS THERE

If one has not given everything, one has given nothing.

Captain Georges Guynemer, French Air Force[16]

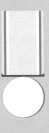

DID YOU KNOW?

One of the most senior Nazi figures of the Second World War flew in the war. Hermann Goering was a successful pilot, shooting down twenty-two Allied aircraft and taking command of the JG 1 wing when Manfred von Richthofen was killed. He became Hitler's deputy and head of the German air force.

BRITAIN

Edward 'Mick' Mannock VC
61 kills

Mannock did not fit the stereotypical image of the public schoolboy, 'play the game' Royal Flying Corps pilot. He was a socialist and not averse to speaking his mind. However, like Boelcke, he was respected as a tactician and mentor to younger and inexperienced pilots. Mannock's overwhelming fear was of being burnt alive and he carried a revolver in the cockpit to avoid this. On 26 July 1918, his aircraft caught fire. He was seen struggling in the cockpit to control the aircraft before it crashed. Whether he used his own pistol is not known.

I WAS THERE

Attack everything.

Notice posted by Royal Flying Corps squadron commander
Lanoe Hawker VC on his squadron's notice board

James McCudden VC
57 kills

McCudden began the war as a mechanic and travelled to France in August 1914, but it wasn't until 1916 that he qualified as a pilot. He spent time as a home defence pilot in Britain; however, despite his prowess, he was unable to shoot down any German aircraft or airships. McCudden was known for his professional attitude – he would not charge recklessly into an enemy formation like Albert Ball. If conditions were not to his advantage, McCudden would withdraw. He died in a simple accident while trying to return to an airfield after suffering an engine failure.

Albert Ball VC
44 Kills

Albert Ball's shyness and boyish demeanour – he arrived at the front aged 19 – belied his fearless approach to combat flying. He often flew on his own and would charge into large enemy formations. In early 1917, Ball, who was by then a household name, wrote in a letter to his parents about starting 'the great game again'. He was killed weeks later. He was described by *Flight* magazine as 'the greatest individual fighter of the day'.

GERMANY

Manfred von Richthofen
80 kills

The top-scoring fighter pilot of the war. His prowess as a combat pilot was made clear when he shot down twenty-one aircraft in one month: the notorious 'Bloody April' of 1917. Richthofen kept trophies: he had silver cups engraved for each kill and had a wall covered with the cut-out strips of fabric featuring serial numbers of the aeroplanes he'd brought down. His last kill was on 20 April 1918. The next day he was shot down by either fire from the ground or a pursuing Sopwith Camel.

Oswald Boelcke
40 kills

Boelcke commanded the first German fighter squadron to form, Jasta 2, in August 1916. It was equipped with Albatros D-series fighters, which helped overcome Allied aerial dominance. Boelcke himself shot down twenty-one Allied aircraft during the Battle of the Somme. He was an inspiring figure, devising fighter tactics and passing them on to his younger pilots, one of whom was Manfred von Richthofen. His rules for air fighting, known as *Dicta Boelcke*, became standard guidelines for fighter pilots. In October 1916, Boelcke died after colliding with a squadron colleague when attacking an Allied formation.

Max Immelmann
15 kills

One of the first aces, he developed an aerobatic move that bears his name – the Immelmann Turn – where the aircraft climbs then reverses direction to make another pass at the target. Germany's highest military medal, the *Pour Le Merite*, was nicknamed the Blue Max after being awarded to Immelmann, who was the first pilot to receive it. When he died in 1916, Royal Flying Corps pilots dropped a wreath over his airfield in tribute.

DID YOU KNOW?

Rock band Led Zeppelin's second album from 1969 features a photograph of the pilots of the famed German Jasta 11 Squadron. The image was edited to include the faces of the four band members plus others, including Apollo 11 astronaut Neil Armstrong.

I WAS THERE

I hope he roasted all the way down.

Mick Mannock on the death of Manfred von Richthofen[17]

LIFE ON A SQUADRON

THE LIFE OF a pilot or observer on a Western Front squadron ranged from the extremes of flying in a dangerous environment, where a terrifying death could be seconds away, to a comfortable life on the ground miles from the front line, far removed from the experiences of those in the trenches.

UNIFORMS

Men in the Royal Flying Corps stood out from the rest of their army colleagues, and not just because of their lifestyle or the work they did. For one thing, they had a different uniform, with a double-breasted tunic nicknamed the 'maternity jacket' because its double-breasted style resembled clothes worn by pregnant women. Some officers preferred to wear the standard army uniforms they'd worn in their previous regiments. Another differing aspect was the badge sewn on to the left breast of the wearers' uniforms: a pair of embroidered wings with the letters 'RFC' for pilots and one wing with the letter 'O' for observers.

ACCOMMODATION

Accommodation for the aircrew would normally be in huts or tents, but at times their quarters could be much more comfortable. One squadron's officers found themselves staying in a chateau and were loath to leave. Even if they were staying in tents, they still appreciated not living in mud-soaked trenches, as many of the pilots and observers had come from infantry units. They were not completely free from danger as airfields were liable to be attacked by German aircraft.

LOSSES

When men were killed, the surviving members of a squadron were not encouraged to mourn in public or share their emotions. There was a policy of 'no empty chairs', i.e. replacements were to be sent to squadrons as soon as possible to prevent members dwelling on missing colleagues. Life – and the war – had to carry on. The 'stiff upper lip' attitude was the norm.

> **DID YOU KNOW?**
> By 1918 a third of Royal Air Force aircrew were Canadian.

DID YOU KNOW?

At the start of the war in 1914 there were only four British squadrons in France. Four years later, in November 1918, there were ninety-nine. If the war had continued, there were plans for the Royal Air Force to have 240 squadrons there.

SOCIAL LIFE

When the opportunity arose, usually through bad weather that grounded the aircraft, the crews could venture into local towns. They would eat, drink and some would look for more physical pleasures. Although most behaved, morals were not so high on the agenda when faced with imminent death.

When off duty on their bases, the aircrew unwound in the mess (though the military class system was maintained, and officers and non-commissioned officers had separate facilities). Songs would be sung around a piano – bawdy and darkly comic about flying and the war – and 'binges', which were alcohol fuelled and after which furniture could end up in pieces, were held to celebrate aerial victories, promotions or men going home. Senior officers saw this as allowing the men to unwind, let off steam and lessen the stress. What might be deemed bad behaviour elsewhere was tolerated as it took place out of sight of other units. Many pilots avoided inebriation if they were flying the next day, well aware of the unpleasantness of flying a dawn patrol with a hangover. One pilot, however, flew with a hip flask filled with rum, to 'warm himself up'.

SPECIALISATIONS

Amongst the aircrew there were two specialisms: pilots and observers. In two-seater aircraft, pilots were responsible for flying while observers had to maintain a lookout for enemy fighters, carry out the artillery observation and send messages to the batteries or operate the reconnaissance cameras. If enemy fighters did attack, the observers had to fire the defensive machine guns. Several observers were very good shots and became aces in their own right. There were occasions when the observers would have to take over the controls and guide their stricken aircraft back to base if the pilot was incapacitated. No observers received the VC in the First World War.

I WAS THERE

Openings in Royal Flying Corps

Men are still urgently required for the Royal Flying Corps, especially textile fitters, as armourers, acetylene welders, carpenters, coppersmiths, motor transport drivers, electricians, engineer fitters, watchmakers and instrument repairers, mechanics having experience of wireless telegraphy, cabinetmakers as riggers, tailors as sailmakers, vulcanisers, and petrol winch drivers and fitters.

Advertisement in The Scotsman[18]

GROUND CREW

The ground crew – the 'backbone of all our efforts', as described by Royal Flying Corps commander Hugh Trenchard – had to ensure there were airworthy machines available each morning. They would work through the night if necessary, which was not easy in unheated hangars. However, this was better than when the aircraft they were working on were parked outside. Many air mechanics got a taste of flying when taken up by their pilots (air experience flights were one way a pilot ensured that his mechanic had done a good job!) and went on to apply for flying training.

DID YOU KNOW?

The Royal Flying Corps were not just based in France or Belgium, but had men and machines in these countries: Belgium, Canada (training units), East Africa, Egypt, France, Italy, Jordan, Macedonia, Mesopotamia, Palestine, Russia, Syria, USA (training units).

SQUADRON ROLES

The squadrons themselves became more specialised. At the start of the war a squadron would carry out whatever was required: reconnaissance, bombing, fighting enemy aircraft, etc., and would have several different types of aircraft. Later, it was thought it would be more beneficial if they concentrated on a particular task, so, for example, 56 Squadron was equipped, and its pilots trained, to be a purely fighter squadron.

The work of the squadrons continued right up until the end. The Royal Air Force bombed the town of Metz on 11 November 1918, the final day of the First World War.

DID YOU KNOW?

Hardit Singh Malik was the first Sikh pilot to fly in the British armed forces. He had his flying helmet adapted so that he could wear his turban.

IN THE AIR

THE FIRST WORLD War was the first conflict to see the sky become a battlefield. Much had to be learnt – most of it the hard way – on how to fight a war in this new environment.

TRAINING

As casualties mounted, there was urgency to replace aircrew losses. At one point in 1917, the average life expectancy of a new Royal Flying Corps pilot or observer on the Western Front was eleven days. One officer noted that his flight of four pilots had been completely replaced three times over within a matter of months.

Flying training was still basic, with little time or opportunity to arm a new flyer with the necessary skills or experience to survive and become an effective combat aviator. A vicious spiral existed in that pilots and observers were sent before they were ready, but became casualties themselves and then needed replacing. Pilots arrived with hardly any flying hours in their logbooks: it was common to have less than twenty hours. Recruits would have their first sight of a machine gun when they arrived at a front-line squadron.

COCKPITS

Pilots and observers sat in unheated open cockpits. To protect against the cold they wore sheepskin-lined boots, gloves, leather jackets and helmets, and goggles were worn to stop engine oil getting into their eyes. Silk scarves helped to prevent chafed necks from the constant twisting and turning to spot enemy aircraft attacking from behind.

TEMPERATURE

No matter the season or weather, the higher the pilots flew, the colder it got, and the bitter cold could make life miserable, no matter how many layers of warm clothing were worn. It was so cold that oil in the machine guns would freeze, rendering the weapons useless. Many opportunities to shoot down the enemy were lost as a result of guns jamming.

DID YOU KNOW?

Naval flyers that ditched in the sea relied on messages sent via carrier pigeon. Several crews were rescued, including one that had been stranded on the water for three days.

Frostbite was common amongst those who had no option but to take their gloves off to adjust equipment. Whale oil was issued to cover any exposed skin but due to the smell it was understandably unpopular. However, an Australian pilot called Sidney Cotton devised one accepted solution. It was an all-in-one suit – the 'Sidcot' – which became the standard flying suit and was used in the Second World War.

As well as the cold, the lack of oxygen was also a factor for crews going above 10,000ft, which was often done in order to gain height advantage over enemy formations. It was not uncommon for fighters to cruise at 20,000ft, but altitude sickness slowed reactions and made men ill and incapable of continuing for long periods. It was not until late in the war that oxygen was provided, although some preferred to fly without the potentially explosive canisters in their machines.

AIRSICKNESS

In the tractor-style aircraft, the pilot and observer sat behind the engine, where they were liable to ingest engine oil. Some aircraft engines used castor oil for lubrication and this led to aircrew suffering from diarrhoea.

Petrol fumes and exhaust gases also gave them dizziness, headaches and drowsiness.

WEAPONRY

In single-seat fighters, Lewis machine-gun ammunition was kept in metal drums. When these had to be changed, the pilot had to stand up, hold the control column between his knees (there being no autopilot) and manually take the empty drum off and replace it. This could have alarming consequences. One pilot, Louis Strange, fell out of his aircraft as he attempted to remove a reluctant drum. His aircraft had turned upside down and he was left hanging on to the magazine drum he had been trying to remove. Luckily he was able to summon enough strength to clamber back inside.

DID YOU KNOW?

One German pilot was so attached to his pet dog that he took it on missions and it sat on a fur rug in the cockpit.

I WAS THERE

We crossed our lines at Albert and went up to Baupume, about twelve miles. We got archied* as soon as we got to Baupume. We dropped our bombs trying for the railway and some stores. Then we lit out for Arras, being heavily shelled. I dodged all over the place and managed to avoid any direct clouts, although they managed to sift a few odds and ends of shells through my machine. I found one shrapnel bullet stuck in the wood ... I followed the road to Doullens and landed OK and got the souvenir bullet.

[*Fired at by anti-aircraft gunfire.]

Second Lieutenant Don Brophy, diary entry, Saturday, 1 July 1916[19]

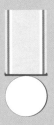

I WAS THERE

Keep You Warm At 20,000 Feet Up

The flying suit is designed to give you perfect freedom to all movements. It is positively water and windproof, light in weight and exceptionally warm. These points will be appreciated by practical aviators. The 'Sidcot' Flying Suit has seen active service and is the result of experience given to us by a well-known aviator. Specification: The cover is of specially prepared khaki twill interlined rubbered muslin lined mohair. With fur collar. £9 9s. Robinson & Cleaver Ltd, Regent Street, London W1

Magazine advertisement for Sidcot flying suit, 1917[20]

PARACHUTES

One item that was not part of a military aviator's flying kit was a parachute. Despite the first successful jump in Britain taking place in 1912, and the fact that functioning parachutes were already being made and advertised, none were given to British aircrew. It was felt that the bulky chutes could affect the pilot's movement in the small cockpits. However, jumps were made from British aircraft: spies used parachutes to drop behind enemy lines. Balloon observers used parachutes; around 750 successful jumps were made. Meanwhile, German pilots were issued with them in 1918 and around forty were saved by their use in the final months.

BRAVERY IN THE AIR

IT TOOK A brave person just to get into an aircraft of the First World War, never mind fly one into battle. The machines were flimsy, prone to structural failure and had engines that were underpowered and which regularly cut out. The art of designing and building successful military aircraft was still in its infancy and aircraft went into service with inbuilt flaws. Aircraft like the BE.2c were cumbersome and regarded as death traps, being unable to escape from predatory enemy fighters. Even later designs like the Sopwith Camel were notoriously tricky to fly and could flick into a spin at a moment's notice. When enemy fire was taken into consideration – aircraft had no armour protection – the bravery of the aircrews is unquestionable.

OFFENSIVE ACTION

There were strong demands on airmen. The commander of the Royal Flying Corps, Hugh Trenchard, was of the mindset similar to army commanders like Field Marshal Douglas Haig, who insisted on an aggressive policy of taking the war to the Germans. Royal Flying Corps aircraft were ordered to dominate the skies above the battlefield, venturing over enemy territory on a regular basis. This put Allied airmen at a disadvantage, however, as if they were hit or suffered technical failures they had to fly over enemy-held ground to get to their own lines. The prevailing winds coming from the west also slowed their return journeys. If they landed short they were lost as prisoners, a problem that did not affect the Germans as much. Indeed, the Germans were happy to allow this constant intrusion into their airspace. Manfred von Richthofen, in his book *The Red Battle Flyer*, menacingly described this policy thus: 'It is better that one's customers come to one's shop'.

EFFECTS

The longer the war continued, the more the long-term effects of flying in combat became apparent. It was not unusual for men to fly two or three times a day and they would develop nervous tics, uncontrollable shaking, stammering and suffer fits of depression and rapid mood swings. British pilots talked of having the 'wind-up' – showing signs of nerves. Some would become full of a quiet fatalism, similar to men in the trenches, awaiting their 'turn'. There was no solace in sleep, with it being interrupted by terrible nightmares of seeing men burning in 'flamers' – planes plummeting to earth on fire.

Even the top aces were not immune. French pilot Georges Guynemer told a friend, 'I shall not survive',[21] and Mick Mannock was constantly plagued by fear and suffered acute anxiety attacks. He managed to overcome them and continued to fly and fight, as did many, but some weren't able to continue. Sympathy was extended by fellow squadron members to genuine cases and men would be transferred back home, to training units as instructors. The acute cases were hospitalised.

FOR VALOUR

Amongst the everyday, dogged courage shown by the airmen, there were exceptional instances of bravery in the air. These three saw Victoria Crosses, Britain's highest military award, being awarded.

DID YOU KNOW?
Nineteen Victoria Crosses were awarded to pilots of the British air services.

William Rhodes-Moorhouse

In the middle of the Battle of Ypres in April 1915, Rhodes-Moorhouse was given the task of bombing Courtrai's railway yards, where thousands of German troops were arriving for the front. He was warned not to fly low, but in order to ensure his bomb landed in the right place, he descended to just 300ft. This brought him well within range of every enemy weapon in the area and, as he turned for home, he was hit, being wounded in the leg, abdomen and hand. Determined to report back, he carried on flying and managed to reach base. After giving his report of the mission he said, 'If I must die, give me a drink.'[22] He was posthumously awarded the Victoria Cross – the first to be given to a British airman.

DID YOU KNOW?

William Rhodes-Moorhouse's son, also called William, served in the Royal Air Force during the Second World War, flying Hurricanes. In the Battle for France, in 1940, he flew from the same airfield as his father had on his last mission. William was shot down and killed during the Battle of Britain.

I WAS THERE

For most conspicuous and consistent bravery from 25 April to 6 May 1917 during which period Captain Ball took part in 26 combats in the air and destroyed 11 hostile aeroplanes, drove down two out of control and forced several others to land. In these combats Captain Ball, flying alone, on one occasion fought six hostile machines, twice he fought five and once four. When leading two other British aeroplanes he attacked an enemy formation of eight. On each of these occasions he brought down at least one enemy. Several times his aeroplane was badly damaged, once so seriously that but for the most delicate handling, his machine would have collapsed, as nearly all the control wires had been shot away. On returning with a damaged machine he had always to be restrained from immediately going out on another. In all, Captain Ball has destroyed 43 German aeroplanes and one balloon, and has always displayed most exceptional courage, determination and skill.

Citation for Victoria Cross[23]

Lionel W.B. Rees

Over the Western Front on 1 July 1916, Rees attacked a formation of ten German bombers. So successful was his solo intervention that the raiders abandoned their mission; in panic, one aircraft's crew jettisoned their bombs over their own troops. Rees was hit in the leg, an injury that ended his combat flying career.

Richard Bell Davies

In November 1915, Royal Naval Air Service Squadron Commander Bell Davies led a bombing raid on a Bulgarian railway junction. One of the attacking aircraft was hit and crash-landed. As Bulgarian troops moved in, Bell Davies landed beside the downed aircraft and the pilot jumped on board. There was an immediate problem: Davies' Nieuport was a single seater. This was overcome as the rescued pilot squeezed into a small space in the fuselage in front of the cockpit, and although his return journey was cramped, he was safely returned back to base.

I WAS THERE

To the memory of Captain Boelcke, our brave and chivalrous foe.

Inscription on wreath dropped over enemy lines by the Royal Flying Corps following the German ace's death

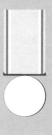

PLANES AT SEA

AS WITH THE army, British navy commanders were not hugely enthusiastic proponents of aviation. The Royal Navy was the strongest in the world and admirals felt that aircraft had little to offer, but Royal Naval Air Servicemen were to achieve many notable successes in naval aviation.

AIRSHIPS

It did not help encourage confidence in aviation when the first naval airship, *Mayfly*, was damaged beyond repair before it could make its maiden flight in 1911 – leading the politician in charge of the Royal Navy, Winston Churchill, to call the 500ft-long craft the 'Won't Fly'. Following this embarrassing incident, the navy cooled their interest in lighter-than-air flying machines for a while to focus on the winged variety. Airships were later developed to carry out coastal patrols and convoy escort duties. Showing the ingenuity that was a mark of the Royal Naval Air Service, one type took the form of a single hydrogen gasbag with an aircraft fuselage slung underneath. By the end of the war 400 airships had been used by the navy.

SEAPLANES

Airships had their uses, but they could not combat enemy airships and they were limited in performance. Aircraft were needed. Britain's first seaplane had taken to the air in November 1911. The aircraft, an Avro type D biplane with floats added under the wings, was piloted by a navy officer with an appropriate-sounding name: Commander Schwann. His experimental work was financed by his fellow officers and their wives, reflecting the official disinterest.

SEAPLANE CARRIERS

Early seaplanes did not have the range needed and a means was needed to take them closer to the action. In January 1912, an aircraft flew from a Royal Navy ship for the first time when a Short S.27 biplane took off from a specially constructed track on top of the battleship HMS *Africa*'s front deck.

More ships were converted to carry seaplanes, including HMS *Hermes*, a navy cruiser, and civilian ships such as *Campania*, an ex-Cunard liner. A merchant ship was given the famous name *Ark Royal*. It could carry ten

DID YOU KNOW?

At first, aircraft that could land on sea were called hydro-aeroplanes but Winston Churchill disliked this term and insisted they be called seaplanes.

seaplanes on its 352ft-long deck, and *Ark Royal* took part in the Gallipoli offensive. However, its seaplanes, which were to carry out artillery observation missions, were unable to climb high enough in the hot conditions to fly above enemy gunfire.

These early carriers used a far from satisfactory method of operation. Seaplanes were lowered to the sea before take-off and then after flight they would land next to the ship and be lifted back on board by crane. Choppy seas would mean cancelled operations as the aircraft were unable to take off or be recovered safely. The machines also weren't sturdy enough and could be smashed to pieces by heavy waves. In addition, a stationary ship was an easier target for German ships or U-boats.

I WAS THERE

It is the work of a lunatic.

Royal Navy admiral on the Mayfly airship[24]

DID YOU KNOW?

In July 1914 – a month before the First World War started – the Royal Naval Air Service had fifty-two seaplanes, forty aircraft and seven airships. Only half the seaplanes were in flyable condition.

CUXHAVEN RAID

On Christmas Eve 1914, Britain was bombed for the first time when a German seaplane attacked Dover. The following day, it was the British seaplanes' turn to attack. Seven were hoisted on to the sea from three carriers before taking off and flying towards Germany, their target the airship base at Cuxhaven. They were unable to hit the sheds but damage was done to installations nearby. It was the first strategic air raid carried out by aircraft operating from ships.

TORPEDO SUCCESS

Another first was chalked up by the Royal Naval Air Service when the first use of air-launched torpedoes was seen in 1915 when Short seaplanes sank several Turkish boats at Gallipoli. Despite the success, these were the first and last torpedo attacks by British aircraft in the First World War.

FLYING BOATS

With seaplanes vulnerable to heavy sea conditions, something sturdier was required and it came in the shape of flying boats. Their boat-like hull allowed them to operate in rougher sea conditions. The most successful British type was the Felixstowe F.2a, a twin-engined biplane developed by Royal Naval Air Service officer John C. Porte from an American Curtiss design. F.2as had seven machine guns and could carry 460lb of bombs. They and other flying boats successfully patrolled the North Sea, destroying several Zeppelins and U-boats. Just as vitally, their presence prevented U-boats from operating with the freedom they would have liked.

AIRCRAFT CARRIERS

The Zeppelins carried out much reconnaissance of the British fleet, but when they ascended to their maximum altitude it was only non-seaplane fighter aircraft that could reach them. Short notice was often given of their approach and so the fleet needed to have fighters on hand to launch quickly. They would take too long to arrive if flying from their land bases so large aircraft carriers were ordered. HMS *Vindex*, a converted Isle of Man passenger ship, saw the first fighter launched from a carrier in late 1915. However, it wasn't until 1917 that a fighter plane was able to land on a moving ship, when Lieutenant Commander E.H. Dunning brought his Sopwith Pup down on to the deck of HMS *Furious*' flat deck. Men on the deck had to catch hold of the plane to stop it, as it had no brakes or other means of stopping itself. Five days later, Dunning's engine failed in another test flight and he was drowned.

HMS *Furious* was not just a test ship, and in July 1918 it launched seven Sopwith Camels for a successful raid on the Tondern Zeppelin base. Two airships were destroyed in the first raid by land-based aircraft operating at sea.

I WAS THERE

In this matter of aerial work for the navy the whole period of the war was a period of experiment rather than achievement.

Walter Raleigh, author of The War in the Air[25]

OTHER INNOVATIONS

It took a long time to build aircraft carriers. HMS *Argus*, a converted Italian liner, fitted with a full-length flush deck to allow aircraft both to take off and land, only entered service one month before the war ended. Meanwhile, the world's first purpose-built aircraft carrier (given the name HMS *Hermes* following the ship of that name's sinking in 1914) wasn't launched until September 1919.

Other methods were needed quickly to allow fighters to attack Zeppelins from the sea. One was barges towed behind destroyers. Lieutenant Stuart D. Culley shot down Zeppelin L.53 in August 1918 after launching from a towed barge in the North Sea. Another method was from platforms built on top of ships' gun turrets, which could turn into the wind to allow easier take-offs. If the wind conditions were right, aircraft would lift off in a distance only twice their length. It was a risky endeavour: the pilots had no way of landing back on their ships and, if out of range of airfields, had to ditch. Then they would hopefully be picked up by a friendly ship. Nevertheless, several airships were shot down from aircraft launched in this way.

NOTES

1. *The Scotsman*, 12 August 1913.
2. Hallion, Richard, *Taking Flight: Inventing the Aerial Age, from Antiquity Through the First World War* (Oxford: Oxford University Press, 2003), p.310.
3. *The Scotsman*, 28 May 1913.
4. Boyne, Walter J., *The Influence of Air Power upon History* (Barnsley: Pen & Sword, 2005), p.58.
5. Ibid., p.65.
6. *The Times*, 29 November 1916.
7. Raleigh, Walter, *The War in the Air: Being the Story of the Part Played in the Great War by the Royal Air Force*, vol. 1 (Oxford: The Clarendon Press, 1922), p.412.
8. McCudden, James, *Flying Fury: Five Years in the Royal Flying Corps* (Oxford: Casemate, 2009), p.200.
9. 'British Air Work – A French Tribute', *Flight*, 12 October 1916, p.890.
10. Taken from J.M. Bruce's article, 'The Sopwith Pup'.
11. Driver, Hugh, *Studies in History. The Birth of Military Aviation: Britain 1903-1914* (Woodbridge: The Boydell Press, 1997), p.95.

12. Taken from J.M. Bruce's article, 'The Sopwith Pup'.

13. Bruce, J.M., 'The FE.2 Series', *Flight*, 12 December 1952, p.725.

14. 'Eddies', article in *Flight*, 5 February 1915, p.9.

15. McCudden, op. cit., p130.

16. Clark, Alan, *Aces High: The War in the Air over the Western Front 1914-18* (George Weidenfeld and Nicolson, 1974), p.103.

17. Ibid., p.131.

18. Advertisement in *The Scotsman*, January 1917.

19. Greenhous, Brereon (ed.), *Rattle of Pebbles: the First World War Diaries of Two Canadian Airmen*, (Minister of Supply and Services Canada, 1987), p.85.

20. *Flight*, 4 October 1917.

21. Guttman, Jon, Osprey Aircraft of the Aces 47.SPAD XII/XIII Aces of World War I (Oxford: Osprey, 2002), p.13.

22. Mackersey, Ian, *No Empty Chairs: The Short and Heroic Lives of the Young Aviators Who Fought and Died in the First World war* (London: Hachette, 2012), p.39.

23. Supplement to the *London Gazette*, 8 June 1917.

24. Jones, H.A., *The War in the Air: Being the Story of the Part Played in the Great War by the Royal Air Force*, vol. 2 (Oxford: Clarendon Press, 1928), p.357.

25. Raleigh, op. cit., p.161.

BIBLIOGRAPHY

Barker, Ralph, *A Brief History of the Royal Flying Corps in World War I* (Robinson, 2002)

Boyne, Walter J., *The Influence of Air Power Upon History* (Pen & Sword Books, 2005)

Bruce, J.M., 'The Sopwith Pup' in *Flight* (1954)

Carey, Louis S. & Batchelor, John, *Naval Aircraft 1914–1939: Purnell's History of the World Wars Special* (Phoebus 1977)

Castle, Ian, *The Zeppelin Base Raids – Germany 1914* (Osprey Publishing, 2011)

Cole, Christopher & Cheesman, E.F., *The Air Defence of Britain, 1914–1918* (Putnam, 1984)

Finnis, Bill, *The History of the Fleet Air Arm: From Kites to Carriers* (Airlife, 2000)

Galdorisi, George & Phillips, Thomas, *Leave No Man Behind: The Saga of Combat Search and Rescue* (Zenith Press, 1999)

Gould Lee, Arthur, *No Parachute: A Classic Account of War in the Air in WWI* (Grub Street, 2013)

Greenhous, Brereon (ed.), *Rattle of Pebbles: the First World War Diaries of Two Canadian Airmen* (Minister of Supply and Services Canada, 1987)

Guttman, Jon, *Osprey Aircraft of the Aces 47: SPAD XII/XIII Aces of World War I* (Osprey Publishing, 2002)

Hart, Peter, *Aces Falling: War Above the Trenches 1918* (Weidenfeld & Nicolson, 2007)

Kershaw, Andrew (ed.), *Fighters of World War One: Purnell's History of the World Wars Special* (Phoebus, 1976)

Levine, Joshua, *Fighter Heroes of WWI* (Collins, 2008)

Lewis, Cecil, *Sagittarius Rising* (Frontline, 2009)

Lawson, Eric & Jane, *The First Air Campaign: August 1914– November 1918* (Da Capo Press, 2002)

Mackersey, Ian, *No Empty Chairs: The Short and Heroic Lives of the Young Aviators who Fought and Died in the First World War* (Weidenfeld & Nicolson, 2012)

March, Daniel J. & Heathcott, John, *The Aerospace Encyclopaedia of Air Warfare*, Vol. 1, 1911–45 (Airtime Publishing, 1997)

Munson, Kenneth, *Aircraft of World War I* (Ian Allan, 1967)

Pollard, Bridget, *The Royal Naval Air Service in Antwerp, September–October 1914* (British Commission for Military History, 2013)

Preston, Antony, *Aircraft Carriers* (Bison Books, 1979)

Raleigh, Walter & Jones, H.A., *The War in the Air: Being the Story of the Part Played in the Great War by the Royal Air Force*, Vols 1–6 (The Clarendon Press, 1922–37)

Rawlings, John D.R., *Pictorial History of the Fleet Air Arm* (Ian Allan, 1973)

Reese, Peter, *The Flying Cowboy: Samuel Cody – Britain's First Airman* (Tempus, 2006)

Spick, Mike, *The Complete Fighter Ace: All the World's Fighter Aces, 1914–2000* (Greenhill, 1999)

Stanton, Robert H., *A Lifetime of Service 1918–1983* (Seagull SA, 1983)

Taylor, John W.R., *Pictorial History of the RAF*, Vol. 1, 1918–39 (Ian Allan, 1968)

Townshend Bickers, Richard, *Von Richthofen: The Legend Evaluated* (Airlife, 1996)

von Richthofen, Captain Manfred, *The Red Battle Flyer* (Robert M. McBride & Co, 1918)

Websites

RAF Museum: www.rafmuseum.org.uk

Flight magazine: www.flightglobal.com

USAF Museum: www.nationalmuseum.af.mil

History Net: www.historynet.com

The Aerodrome: www.theaerodrome.com

The National Archives: www.nationalarchives.gov.uk

Discover more books in this series ...

978-0-7509-5567-6   £5.00

978-0-7509-5452-4   £5.00

978-0-7524-9322-0   £5.00

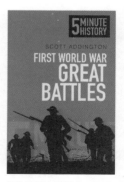

978-0-7524-9321-3   £5.00

Visit our website and discover thousands
of other History Press books.

www.thehistorypress.co.uk